Vecellio's RENAISSANCE COSTUME BOOK

ALL 500 WOODCUT ILLUSTRATIONS FROM THE FAMOUS
SIXTEENTH-CENTURY COMPENDIUM OF WORLD COSTUME

BY CESARE VECELLIO

4318

DOVER PUBLICATIONS, INC., NEW YORK

CONTENTS

Original colophon.

Published in Canada by General Publishing Company, Ltd.,
30 Lesmill Road, Don Mills, Toronto, Ontario.
Published in the United Kingdom by Constable and Company, Ltd., 10 Orange Street, London WC2H 7EG.

Vecellio's Renaissance Costume Book, first published by Dover
Publications, Inc., in 1977, contains all 500 woodcut illustrations from Cesare Vecellio's *Habiti antichi, et moderni di
tutto il Mondo*, printed by Giovanni Bernardo Sessa, Venice,
1598 (this was the second enlarged edition of the work that
originally appeared under the title *De gli Habiti antichi et
moderni di Diverse Parti del Mondo*, printed by Damian
Zenaro, Venice, 1590; see Publisher's Note for further bibliographical details).
The Italian and Latin text of the 1598 edition is replaced
here by a Publisher's Note and captions in English, all prepared specially for the present edition.

DOVER *Pictorial Archive* SERIES

Vecellio's Renaissance Costume Book belongs to the Dover
Pictorial Archive Series. Up to ten illustrations may be
reproduced on any one project or in any single publication,
free and without special permission. Wherever possible, include a credit line indicating the title of this book, artist and
publisher. Please address the publisher for permission to make
more extensive use of illustrations in this book than that
authorized above.
The reproduction of this book in whole is prohibited.

International Standard Book Number: 0-486-23441-x
Library of Congress Catalog Card Number: 76-55952

Manufactured in the United States of America
Dover Publications, Inc.
180 Varick Street, New York, N.Y. 10014

PUBLISHER'S NOTE

The sixteenth century was the golden age of the costume book. The great wealth of the mercantile classes was reflected not only in conspicuous consumption, clothes being a principal article, but also in a great wave of travel and exploration in search of markets and raw materials, with the concomitant discovery of exotic modes of dress. European artists could not help being inspired by these phenomena, and between 1520 and 1610 over 200 collections of engravings, etchings or woodcuts were published that were concerned with clothing or personal adornment.

In the second half of the century there appeared the first printed books (some hand-painted manuscripts had preceded) that brought together costumes from many parts of the world. The earliest known is Richard Breton's *Recueil de la diversité des habits* (Paris, 1562) with over a hundred illustrations attributed to Enea Vico. Other major universal costume collections were those of Ferdinando Bertelli (Venice, 1563), Jost Amman (Nuremberg, 1577; the woodcuts executed by Hans Weigel), Abraham de Bruyn (Cologne, 1577; the second edition of 1581 contained 79 plates with over 500 costumed figures), Jean-Jacques Boissard (Mechlin, 1581), Bartolomeo Grassi (Rome, 1585), Pietro Bertelli (Padua, 1589, 1591 and 1596) and —the best known of all and in many respects the apex of the century's achievements—that of Cesare Vecellio.

Vecellio, a distant cousin of Titian (Tiziano Vecelli or Vecellio), was born in Pieve di Cadore (in the mountainous Belluno region north of Venice) about 1521 and died in Venice in 1601. He studied painting with Titian's brother Francesco and was acquainted with Titian, whom he accompanied to Augsburg in 1548, when the great painter was commanded by Charles V to attend the Imperial Diet there. Cesare Vecellio never became a prominent painter (his only authenticated works are some church decorations in his native region; the fore-edge paintings of some luxurious books have been attributed to him). His fame rests on

two printed books that he wrote and illustrated: the *Corona delle nobili et virtuose donne* (Venice, 1591), a magnificent collection of lace patterns, and the great costume book.

The first edition of Vecellio's costume work was printed by Damian Zenaro in Venice in 1590 (the preface, transferred without alteration to the second edition, is dated 1589), with the title *De gli Habiti antichi et moderni di Diverse Parti del Mondo*. The 420 woodcut plates were, in all probability, drawn by Vecellio and cut in wood by the Nuremberg-born master Christoph Chrieger (referred to in the text as "Cristoforo Guerra"; Chrieger, who worked with Vecellio on a major print in 1572 and who died in Venice in the late 1580s, may possibly have been the "Cristoforo" who cut the excellent portraits of artists in the famous 1568 edition of Vasari's *Lives*). There were two unequal parts in the first edition, the 361 illustrations in Book I dealing with Europe (including Turkey) and the 59 in Book II surveying Asian and African garb.

Like most of his predecessors, Vecellio emphasized the dress of his own region and arranged his pictures in a sequence moving from close-to-home to far-from-home. But he placed Rome before Venice, no doubt because of its historical priority in Italian life, and in general he was the tentative creator of costume history: his examples of earlier modes of dress (chiefly in the sections on Rome and Venice), largely founded on the study of old works of art preserved in churches and public buildings, were the first ever published, the previous costume authors having portrayed only contemporary dress. Naturally, Vecellio's section on Venice and the Venetian region is the most reliable as well as the largest by far, fascinating not only in its wide range of occupations and social strata, but also in its great diversity of dresses that could be worn by wealthy women according to age and occasion. Vecellio also seems to be offering original material for certain other parts of Italy, such as Naples and Sicily, but he borrowed from Boissard for

Lombardy and Tuscany, as well as for Turkey and the Orient, from Amman for Germany and central Europe, and from Grassi for Flanders and England.

The second edition of Vecellio's book, the basis of the present volume, was called *Habiti antichi, et moderni di tutto il Mondo*, and was printed in Venice by Giovanni Bernardo Sessa in 1598. In this edition, Vecellio omitted most of his introductory historical text and shortened his captions considerably, so that the pictures now appeared on every verso page, with each facing recto occupied by a brief Italian text at the top and a newly prepared Latin translation at the bottom. But, more important, the number of illustrations was increased to 500 (ostensibly 507, but see below). New plates were inserted in many areas of the book (for instance, the Pope and Cardinals, and Prester John and his associates, first appeared in 1598), and a 20-picture section on the New World was added, derived from various travel accounts (our Nos. 489 and 497–500, for example, are redrawn from Theodor de Bry's engravings after John White's drawings for Thomas Harriot's *Briefe and True Report of the New Found Land of Virginia*, Frankfurt, 1590; reprinted by Dover, 1972). It is not known who cut the additional woodblocks.

Although the general sequence of pictures in this 1598 edition corresponded to that in the first edition, the sequence of the individual plates was quite different (the 1598 is followed in the present volume with a few variations for the sake of page layout), and the original two parts became twelve: (1) Italy (our Nos. 1–221), (2) France, Lowlands and Burgundy (our 222–244), (3) Spain and Portugal (245–267), (4) England (268–275), (5) northern Europe (276–299), (6) Germany and central Europe (300–338), (7) Poland and neighboring lands (339–350), (8) European Turkey and Greece (351–383 and 384–399), (9) Hungary and what is now Yugoslavia (400–408), (10) Africa (409–433), (11) Asia (434–480) and (12) America (481–500). Italy, which accounts for nearly half the book, can be further subdivided into: Rome (the Church, 1 & 2; ancient, 3–12; medieval, 13 & 14; "modern"—that is, of Vecellio's time—15–26), Venice and the Venetian region (before 1590, 27–76; "modern," 77–161) and other regions (Lombardy, northwest, Tuscany, center, Naples and Sicily, 162–221).

Our new numeration reflects the actual number of different pictures; the "507" of 1598 included a nonpictorial part title and an exact repetition of certain plates that has not been indicated in the standard bibliographies: our No. 15, "Roman nobleman," was also used by Vecellio as "Modern Milanese nobleman," "Modern Florentine nobleman" and "Modern Neapolitan nobleman," and our No. 21, "Roman merchant," recurred as "Modern Italian merchants," "Modern Florentine merchants" and "Modern Neapolitan merchants"; we run these two figures only once each. Moreover, in the 1590 and 1598 editions, every picture appears within a heavy late-Renaissance frame, but only eight different frames are used repeatedly throughout. In this book we have used the frames once each on the eight part-title pages (see the table of contents for the eight parts into which we have transformed Vecellio's twelve); the original main-title frame is reproduced on the inside back cover. Our illustrations appear in one of two sizes, either 94% or 125% of the originals. Vecellio's text has been replaced by new brief captions in English, which strive to supply the correct modern forms of geographical names and the exact or accepted forms of Turkish nomenclature, but which only occasionally rectify or enlarge upon the indications given by the artist himself.

When *Habiti antichi, et moderni di tutto il Mondo* was reprinted in Venice in 1664, Cesare Vecellio was incorrectly identified as the brother of Titian, and Titian was credited for some of the artwork. That it was generally believed for the next two centuries that the book was Titian's work is a fine compliment to Cesare's achievement. The book, which also appeared in Spanish (Madrid, 1794) and with a French adaptation of the text (Paris, 1859/60; artwork completely redrawn), has always been highly esteemed, and classical actresses like Ellen Terry and Julia Marlowe have found it invaluable for costuming roles. Little wonder, when Vecellio, a contemporary of Shakespeare, can supply, for *Othello* alone: "The Doge," "Venetian general in wartime," "Venetian senators and knights," "Venetian magistrates," "[Venetian] Soldier in noncombat dress" and even "Wife of the governor of a Venetian foreign possession"!

ITALY

1. The Pope.

2. The Cardinals.

3. *Military dress of ancient Roman consuls and tribunes.*

4. *Ancient Roman patrician.*

5. *Roman standard-bearer.*

6. *"Very ancient dress of Romans, used earlier by the Trojans"* [*actually military dress of Roman tetrarchs, ca. 300 A.D.*].

7. *Ancient Roman infantryman.*

9. *Ancient Roman cavalryman.*

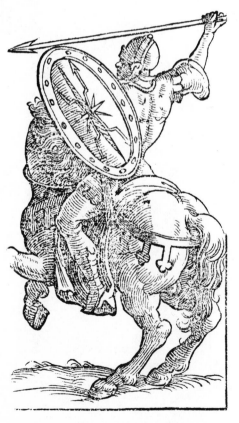

8. *Ancient Roman light cavalryman.*

10. *Ancient Roman light infantryman.*

12. *Ancient Roman slinger.*

11. *Ancient Roman noblewoman wearing the stola.*

13. *Women's garb in Rome and all Italy,*
ca. 1000 A.D.

15. *Roman nobleman [of Vecellio's time].*

14. *Women's garb in Rome and all Italy,*
ca. 1300.

6   ITALY: ROME

16. *Young Roman noblewoman.*

17. *Roman baroness or other noblewoman.*

18. *Festive street attire of young married noblewomen of Rome.*

19. *Street dress of Roman girls and young unmarried women of the nobility.*

20. *Roman widow.*

21. *Roman merchant.*

22. *Roman merchant's wife.*

23. *Roman artisan's wife.*

24. *Special garb of Roman prostitutes in the reign of Pius V (1566–72).*

25. *Current garb of Roman prostitutes.*

26. *Peasant woman of the Roman countryside.*

27. *The first Doge of Venice.*

28. *Another early Doge.*

29. *Medieval Venetian nobleman.*

30. *Another medieval Venetian nobleman.*

31. *Medieval Venetian noblewoman.*

32. *Festive garb of medieval Venetian noblewoman.*

33. *Medieval baron's garb in Venice and all Italy.*

34. *Feudal lord's garb in Venice and all Italy.*

35. *Chatelaine's garb in Venice and all Italy.*

36. *Man wearing the medieval* dogalina [*robe with characteristic sleeves*].

37. *Medieval garb of young nobleman out wooing.*

38. *Medieval garb of young noblewoman being wooed.*

39. Dogalina *for noblewomen's street wear.*

40. *Medieval Venetian noblewoman at home.*

41. *Medieval Venetian noblewoman, at a period later than the* dogalina.

43. *Venetian armor, ca. 1200.*

42. *Man wearing the medieval* dogalina *(Venice and other parts of Italy).*

44. *Young men in the medieval garb of Venice and other parts of Italy.*

45. *Old Venetian costume, apparently the origin of that of Vecellio's day.*

46. *Medieval garb of young men.*

47. *Similar medieval garb of young men.*

48. *Old attire of soldiers and bravos.*

49. *Member of the society known as the* Compagni della calza.

50. *Old costume worn in and around* Venice.

51. *Old costume worn in Venice and other Italian cities.*

52. *Old costume of youths and younger men.*

53. *Costume of young men in Italy around the time of Ezzelino (ca. 1250).*

54. *Armor of the time of Emperor Rudolph I (late 13th century).*

55. *Armor from the latter half of the 15th century.*

56. *Old feminine costume.*

58. *The Doge's wife.*

57. *The Doge [costume of Vecellio's time, but much earlier in origin].*

18   ITALY: VENICE

59. *Old costume of the lords of Carrara and other great lords.*

60. *Old costume of knights in Venetia and Lombardy.*

61. *Costume of Venetian senators, ca. 1400.*

62. *Old costume of Venetian ambassadors sent to Syria and elsewhere.*

63. *Old costume of Venetian noblewomen.*

64. *Old costume of Venetian merchants in Syria.*

65. *Old costume of young married women of Venice.*

66. *Old costume of marriageable maidens.*

67. *Another old costume for unmarried young women.*

68. *More modest "reformed" dress of olden days.*

69. *Venetian costume, ca. 1500.*

70. *Old costume worn in Venice and other parts of Italy.*

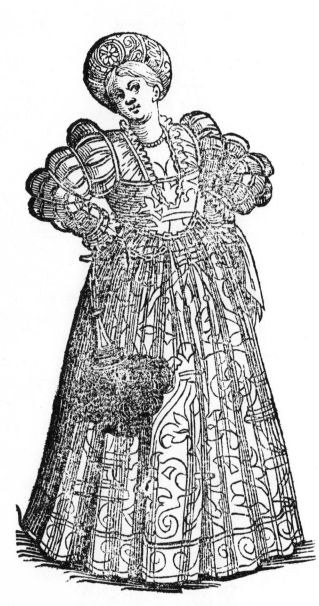

72. *Costume of older and younger married women, ca. 1100.*

71. *Old costume worn in Venice and other parts of Italy.*

73. *Costume of Venetian women, ca. 1530.*

74. *Venetian noblewoman in mourning, 1550.*

76. *Soldier in garrison attire at the time of Emperor Charles V (ca. 1550).*

75. *Costume of Venetian women, 1550.*

77. *Venetian general in wartime [in Vecellio's day].*

78. *Venetian senators and knights.*

79. *Venetian magistrates (the three chiefs of the Council of Ten).*

80. *Ordinary costume of Venetian noblemen.*

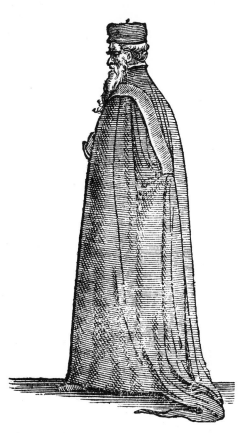

81. *Mourning garb of Venetian noblemen.*

82. *Young Venetian nobleman up to the age of 20.*

83. *Winter garb of Venetian noblemen.*

84. *Domestic garb of Venetian noblemen and wealthy citizens.*

85. *The Great Captain (head of Venetian internal security).*

86. *The subordinate Venetian captains (police officials).*

87. *The Doge's Knight.*

88. *The Doge's 16 squires.*

89. *Venetian merchants and shopkeepers.*

90. *The 50 Venetian public criers.*

91. *The Venetian admiral.*

92. *The masters of the arsenal.*

93. *Unmarried young Venetian woman.*

95. *Street dress of young Venetian women after marriage.*

94. *Venetian bride before her marriage.*

97. *Young married woman of Venice in Ascension holiday costume.*

96. *Young married woman of the Venetian nobility.*

98. *Winter costume of Venetian noblewomen and wealthy ladies.*

99. *Venetian noblewoman dressed for a
public celebration.*

100. *Venetian noblewoman dressed for
visiting S. Pietro di Castello during Lent.*

101. *Venetian widow.*

102. *Wife of the governor of a Venetian foreign possession.*

103. *Elderly Venetian lady.*

104. *Dress of women of non-Venetian origin residing in Venice.*

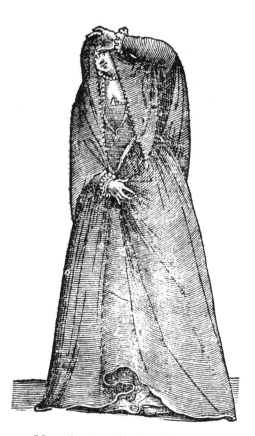

105. *Venetian prostitute outdoors.*

106. *Well-to-do Venetian woman at home.*

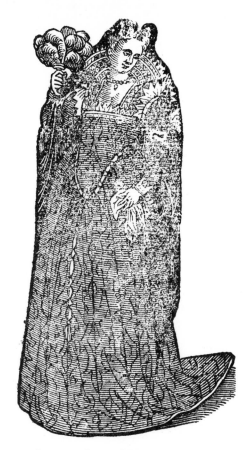

107. *Current dress of Venetian noblewomen.*

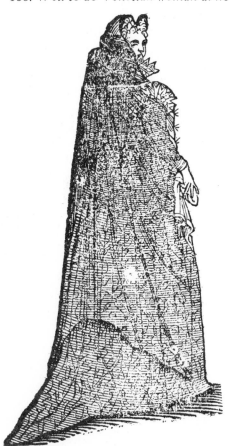

108. *Rear view of a costume similar to the preceding.*

109. *Venetian prostitute in wintertime.*

110. *Winter dress of Venetian women at home and outdoors.*

112. *Venetian woman bleaching her hair in the sun on a rooftop gallery.*

111. *Venetian brothel prostitute.*

113. A pizzochera (*member of a religious society for women*).

114. *Girl from one of the Venetian female orphanages.*

115. *Venetian domestic servant.*

116. *Market gardener from Chioggia or Palestina (near Venice).*

117. *Venetian gondolas.*

118. *Foreign noblemen and dignitaries seen in Venice.*

119. *Rector of the University of Padua.*

120. *Doctors or assessors on the Venetian mainland.*

122. *Doctors of law or medicine in Lombardy.*

121. *Young men and students in Venice.*

123. *Young men in Venice and other parts of Italy.*

124. *Soldier in noncombat dress.*

125. *Infantryman in battle dress.*

126. *Bravos in Venice and other parts of Italy.*

127. *Mourning garb on the Venetian mainland.*

128. *Colonels, knights and captains in mourning.*

129. *Cavalryman in full battle dress.*

130. *Current armor for man and horse.*

131. *Light cavalryman in armor.*

132. Scappoli (*voluntary soldiers on board galleys*).

133. Galeotti or falila (*conscript soldiers on galleys*).

135. *Member of brotherhood who accompany criminals to execution.*

134. *Galley slave.*

136. *Venetian mortician.*

137. *Certain mendicants who seek alms in Venetian churches and streets.*

138. *Venetian porters and stevedores.*

139. *Market porter.*

140. *Peasant woman from outskirts of Venice as seen in town on Ascension Day.*

141. *Young peasant bridegroom at a celebration.*

142. *Peasant woman from the Treviso area.*

143. *Peasant in a Venetian market.*

144. *Piazzetta di S. Marco, looking from the Canal toward the Basilica.*

145. *Piazza S. Marco, looking toward the main façade of the Basilica.*

44   ITALY: VENICE

146. *Piazza and Piazzetta di S. Marco,*
looking toward S. Giorgio.

147. *Courtyard of the Doge's Palace.*

148. *Bride from the Friuli region.*

150. *Noblewoman from Cividale.*

149. *Domestic attire of noblewomen in Cividale del Friuli.*

151. *Former costume of citizens of Cividale and other parts of Italy.*

152. *Peasant woman from Cividale.*

153. *Noblewoman from Conegliano.*

154. *Old costume for men and women in Padua.*

155. *Current dress of Paduan noblewomen.*

156. *Young married woman of Padua.*

157. *Paduan matron.*

158. *Woman of Vicenza.*

159. *Noblewomen of Brescia, Verona and other cities near Lombardy.*

160. *Matrons of Verona and Brescia.*

161. *Noblewoman of Brescia.*

162. *Old costume of Milanese women.*

163. *Noblewomen and ladies of Milan and elsewhere in Lombardy.*

164. *Noble matrons of Milan and elsewhere in Lombardy.*

165. *Another costume of Milan and elsewhere in Lombardy.*

166. *The Duchesses of Parma and other great ladies in Italy.*

167. *Matrons and important ladies of Parma.*

169. *Chief noblewomen of Lombardy.*

168. *Some noblewomen of Lombardy.*

170. *Woman of moderate means.*

171. *Peasant and lower-class girls of Parma.*

172. *Matron of Turin.*

173. *Girl of Turin.*

175. *Old feminine costume of Genoa and Liguria in general.*

174. *Current Genoese noblewoman.*

176. *Genoese woman of the poorer classes.*

178. *Principal magistrates of Florence.*

177. *Grand Duke of Tuscany.*

179. *Ordinary dress of Florentine noblemen.*

180. *Chief matrons of Florence.*

181. *Old feminine costume of Tuscany, ca. 1300.*

182. *Young noble bride in Florence and other parts of Tuscany.*

183. *Young Florentine woman married for some years.*

184. *Obsolete street dress of Florentine girls.*

185. *Current dress of unmarried Tuscan noblewomen.*

186. *Tuscan women of 30 to 45 years of age.*

187. *Women's attire common in Florence and in Lombardy.*

188. *Florentine widows and women in mourning.*

189. *Peasants in Florence and Tuscany in general.*

190. *Unmarried peasant woman of Tuscany.*

192. *Wives of Sienese city officials.*

191. *Noble matron of Siena.*

193. *Woman of Perugia.*

194. *Noble matron of Pisa.*

195. *Girls and unmarried women of Pisa.*

196. *Noblewoman of Bologna.*

197. *Unmarried noblewoman of Bologna on her way to church.*

198. *Prostitute of Bologna.*

199. *Noble matron of Mantua.*

200. *Young unmarried noblewoman of Mantua.*

201. *Another costume of Mantuan noble matrons.*

202. *Unmarried woman of Ferrara.*

203. *Street dress of matron of Ferrara.*

204. *Women of Romagna and part of the Marche.*

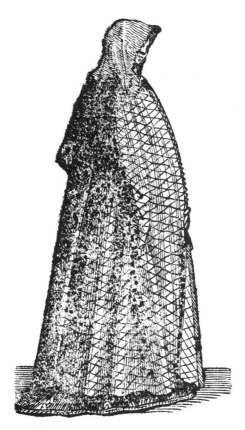

205. *Woman of Ancona.*

206. *Old feminine costume of Naples, ca.
1400.*

208. *Neapolitan matron.*

207. *Neapolitan baroness.*

209. *Obsolete feminine costume of Naples.*

211. *Current costume of Neapolitan matrons.*

210. *Neapolitan girl.*

213. *Current costume of Neapolitan noblewomen.*

212. *Noblewoman of rank in the Kingdom of Naples.*

214. *Neapolitan noble matron in summertime.*

215. *Neapolitan unmarried noblewoman.*

216. *Man of Calabria.*

217. *Woman of Gaeta.*

218. *Woman of the island of Ischia.*

220. *Sicilian noblewoman in church.*

219. *Noble matron of Sicily dressed for a public festivity.*

221. *Young unmarried Sicilian noblewoman going to church.*

66   ITALY: KINGDOM OF NAPLES AND SICILY

FRANCE,
SPAIN AND
ENGLAND

222. *King of France.*

223. *Old feminine French attire.*

224. *Young married Frenchwoman of the
nobility.*

225. *Noble matrons of Paris and vicinity.*

226. *Noble matron of Orléans.*

227. *Noblewoman of Avignon.*

228. *Unmarried French noblewoman.*

229. *French noblewoman in mourning.*

230. *French nobleman.*

231. *Girls of Antwerp and Brabant.*

232. *Noblewoman of Antwerp.*

234. *Noblewomen of Antwerp and Brabant.*

233. *Woman of Brabant.*

235. *Nobleman of Holland.*

236. *Matron of Holland.*

237. *Girl of Metz.*

238. *Obsolete costume of French noblemen.*

239. *Burgundian nobleman.*

240. *Current French male costume.*

241. *Court costume of French noble matron.*

242. *Woman of Verdun.*

243. *Woman of Lorraine.*

244. *Woman of Vaudémont (Lorraine).*

246. *Old feminine costume of Spain.*

245. *King of Spain (Philip II).*

247. *Court costume of Spanish noblemen.*

248. *Noble matron of Spain.*

249. *Widowed Spanish noblewoman.*

250. *Spanish noblewoman at a public festivity.*

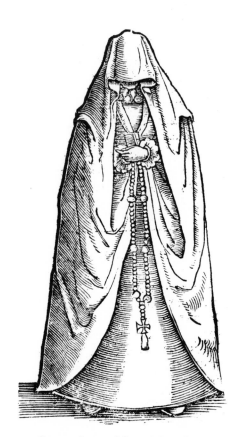

251. *Street dress of Spanish girls.*

252. *Spanish unmarried woman.*

253. *Spanish noble matron.*

254. *Woman of Toledo.*

255. *Woman of Santander.*

256. *Woman of Bilbao.*

257. *Woman of the Spanish Basque provinces.*

258. *Lower-class Basque woman.*

259. *Man of Granada.*

261. *Girl of Granada.*

260. *Woman of Granada.*

262. *Man of Portugal.*

264. *Man of Galicia (Spain).*

263. *Portuguese matron.*

266. *Man of Navarra.*

265. *Matron of Galicia.*

267. *Woman of Navarra.*

268. *English noble matron.*

269. *English nobleman.*

270. *English girl.*

272. *Young Englishman.*

271. *English merchant.*

274. *English widow.*

273. *English noblewoman.*

275. *English sailor.*

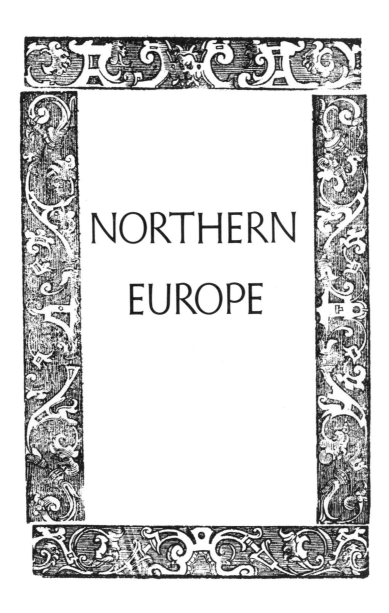

NORTHERN

EUROPE

276. *The Grand Duke of Muscovy.*

277. *Ancient Gothic cavalryman.*

278. *Young married women of Lolland [Livonia?], Gotland and Öland.*

279. *Swedish matron.*

280. *Young married women of the Norwegian nobility.*

281. *Women of Götaland.*

282. *Young married woman of Lolland.*

283. *Girl of Lolland.*

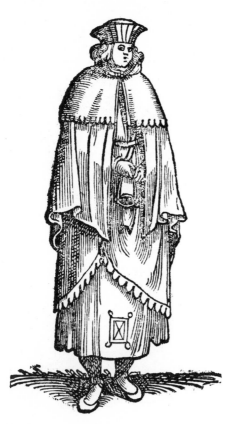

284. Lower-class women of Lolland and Gotland.

285. Man of Norway.

286. Northern woman with torches for the Arctic night.

287. Man of the northern regions on a journey.

288. *Man of "Biarmia" (Arctic region).*

289. *Woman of "Biarmia."*

290. *Man and woman of "Scrifinia" (between "Biarmia" and Finland).*

291. *Man of "Scrifinia."*

292. *Laplander.*

293. *Young married woman of Lapland.*

294. *Christian woman of the northern regions bringing her children to a remote church for baptism.*

295. *Sleighs of the northern regions.*

296. *Noble Muscovite ambassador.*

297. *Woman of Muscovy.*

298. *Muscovite infantryman in battle dress.*

299. *Muscovite cavalryman.*

GERMANY
AND
CENTRAL
EUROPE

300. *Holy Roman Emperor.*

301. *Clerical elector of the Empire.*

302. *Lay elector of the Empire.*

303. *German princes or barons.*

304. *Titled German nobleman.*

305. *Old costume of German women, ca. 1400.*

306. *Tyrolean noblewoman.*

307. *Young noblewoman of Augsburg.*

308. *Young patrician woman of Augsburg.*

309. *Noble matron of Augsburg.*

310. *Nobleman of Bohemia.*

311. *Bohemian commoner.*

312. *Noblewoman of Bohemia.*

313. *Bohemian woman of the people.*

314. *Well-to-do Swiss.*

315. *Swiss girl.*

316. *Swiss matron.*

317. *Alsatian woman.*

318. *Alsatian man.*

320. *Senators and other leading citizens of Leipzig.*

319. *German carter.*

321. *Merchant of the Netherlands.*

322. *Bavarian matron.*

323. *Girl from Nuremberg.*

324. *Nuremberg bride.*

325. *Nuremberg bride of the nobility.*

326. *Nuremberg matron in festive attire.*

328. *Noblewoman of the Palatinate.*

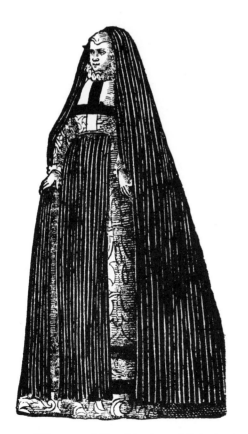

327. *Woman of Frankfurt am Main in street dress.*

329. *Noblewoman of Cologne.*

330. *Matron of Cologne.*

331. *Noble matron of Alsace.*

332. *Young married women of Meissen and Saxony in general.*

334. *Girl of Meissen in festive attire.*

333. *Silesian bride on her way to church.*

335. *Noblewoman of Meissen.*

336. *Middle-class Silesian woman.*

337. *Unmarried Silesian woman.*

338. *Servant girls of Danzig, Pomerania or Denmark.*

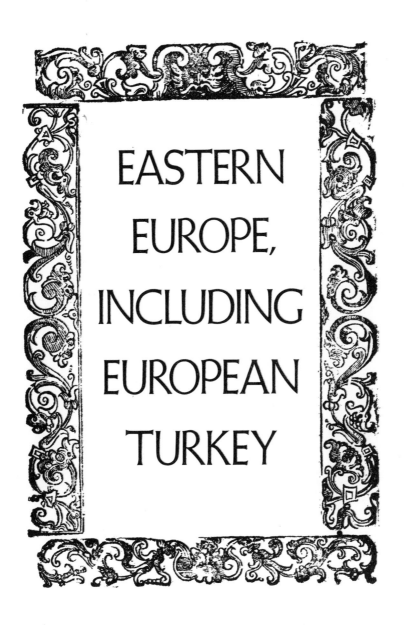

EASTERN
EUROPE,
INCLUDING
EUROPEAN
TURKEY

339. *King of Poland.*

340. *Pole.*

341. *Prussian merchant.*

342. *Woman of Poznań.*

343. *Women of Poland, Prussia or Muscovy.*

344. *Young married woman of Danzig.*

346. *Well-to-do Lithuanian woman.*

345. *Northern Russian.*

347. *Lithuanian.*

348. *Lithuanian woman from Grodno.*

349. *Noblewoman of Livonia.*

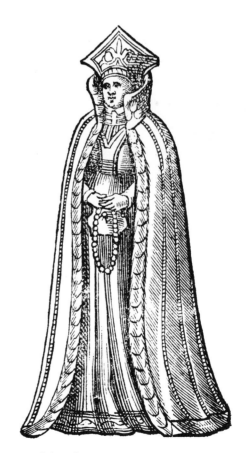

350. *Livonian woman.*

EASTERN EUROPE: BALTIC REGION   109

351. *The Sultan of Turkey.*

352. *A mufti, Moslem religious jurist.*

353. *The aga, general of the Janizaries.*

354. *A bölük paşa, officer of Janizaries.*

355. A cadilesker, one of the two chief judges.

356. A titled Turk at home.

357. A kapıcı, or palace doorkeeper.

358. Turkish rider in rainy weather.

359. A peyk, *one of the 40 royal lackeys.*

361. A Janizary.

360. An archer of the Sultan's guard.

362. *Well-to-do Turkish woman in street attire.*

363. *A Turkish principal wife riding through the streets.*

364. *Turkish woman at home.*

365. *The favorite of the Sultan.*

366. *Woman of the harem.*

367. *Middle-class Turkish woman.*

368. The beglerbeg (*Turkish provincial governor*) *of Greece.*

369. *The* beglerbeg *of Anatolia, and other armored soldiers.*

370. *An* azab, *or marine (galley archer).*

371. *Artilleryman.*

372. *Slaves and pages of the Sultan.*

373. *Turkish bravos, followers of pashas and beglerbegs.*

374. *Turkish independent bravos.*

375. *Slaves of the pashas.*

376. An acemi oğlan *(recruit in the Janizaries; or else, boy conscripted for labor).*

378. *Turkish pirate.*

377. *Turkish hired servant.*

379. *Turkish woman.*

380. *Turkish burial.*

381. *Fakir, or Moslem holy mendicant.*

382. *Dervish, one of an order of religious mendicants.*

383. *A "Frank" (Western European merchant in Constantinople or elsewhere in Turkey).*

384. *The Greek Patriarch of Constantinople.*

385. *Greek monk.*

386. *Rear view of a Greek monk.*

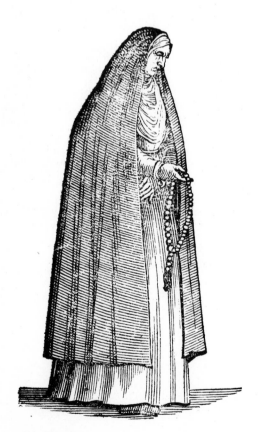

387. *Greek nun.*

388. *Greek nobleman.*

389. *Greek merchant.*

390. *Greek married woman of Pera.*

391. *Greek woman of Pera.*

392. *Greek woman in the Venetian domain.*

393. *Man of Sphakia in Crete.*

395. *Woman of Sphakia in Crete.*

394. *Young noblewoman of Macedonia.*

396. *Macedonian matron.*

397. *Married woman of Saloniki.*

398. *Woman of Mitylene.*

399. *Concubine from Rhodes.*

400. *The Prince of Transylvania.*

401. *Croats, Hungarians, Poles.*

402. *Hungarian and Croatian noblemen.*

404. *Slavonian or Dalmatian man.*

403. *Specifically Hungarian costume.*

405. *Dalmatian or Slavonian woman.*

406. *Chief of the Uskoks.*

407. *Dalmatian woman from the island of Cres.*

408. *Young girl from Dubrovnik.*

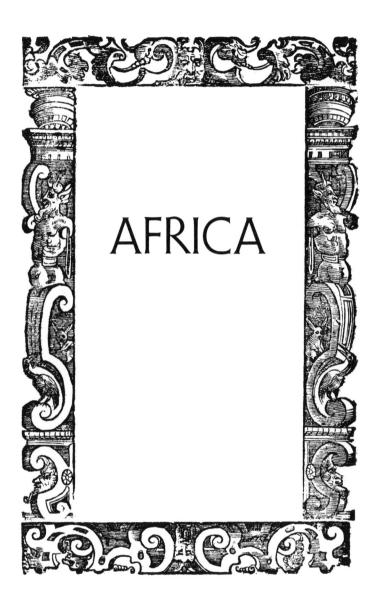

AFRICA

409. *Prester John (legendary Christian ruler of Ethiopia).*

410. *Prester John's pages.*

411. *Prester John's chief assistants.*

413. *Ethiopian girl.*

412. *Ethiopian nobleman.*

415. *Kansuh al-Ghuri (reigned 1501–16), last Sultan of Egypt before the Turkish conquest.*

414. *Ethiopian soldier.*

416. *Admirals and councillors of the Sultan of Egypt.*

418. *Moorish nobleman of Cairo.*

417. *Woman of Cairo.*

419. *A mameluke (guard of the Sultan).*

420. *An Indian Christian in Cairo.*

422. *Moorish girl.*

421. *Berber nobleman.*

423. *Well-to-do Moor.*

424. *North African woman.*

425. *Black inhabitant of North Africa.*

426. *Man from the Kingdom of Tlemcen.*

428. *Middle-class African woman.*

427. *Woman from Tlemcen.*

429. An "African Indian."

430. "African Indian from Ceffala."

431. *Man from the African kingdom of "Giabea."*

433. *Attire of some of the black inhabitants of Zanzibar.*

432. *Man from the Canary Islands.*

ASIA

435. *Tartar soldier.*

434. *The Great Khan of the Tartars.*

436. *Former costume of noblewomen of Karamania (in Anatolia), before the Turkish conquest.*

437. *Current costume of Karamanian noblewomen.*

438. *Karamanian woman in Constantinople.*

439. *Well-to-do Karamanian.*

440. *Latest costume of Karamanian women.*

441. *Well-to-do Armenian.*

442. *Armenian merchant.*

443. *Woman of lower Armenia.*

444. *Woman of lower Armenia with a costume emphasizing her chastity.*

445. *Nobleman of lower Armenia.*

447. *The Shah of Persia.*

446. *Georgian.*

448. *Persian woman.*

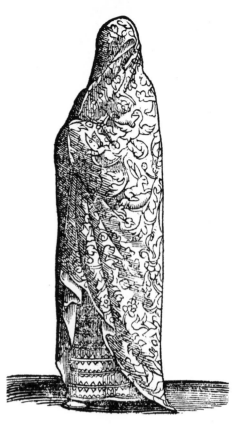

449. *Persian matron.*

450. *Persian nobleman.*

451. *Persian captain.*

452. *Persian girl.*

453. *Another Persian girl.*

454. *Married woman of Persia.*

455. *Persian infantryman.*

456. *Woman of Damascus.*

457. *Woman of Tripoli in Syria.*

458. *Woman of Beirut.*

459. *Noblewoman of Aleppo.*

460. *Syrian matron.*

461. *Girl of Aleppo.*

462. *Married woman of Syria.*

463. *Greek woman in Syria.*

464. *Jewish woman in Syria.*

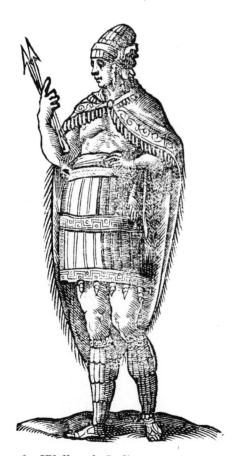

465. *Well-to-do Indian.*

466. *Asian Gypsy woman.*

467. *Well-to-do Indian woman.*

468. *Indian woman of moderate means.*

469. *Woman of the Moluccas.*

470. *Young man of Japan.*

471. Noble matron of China.

472. Chinese noblewoman.

473. Chinese nobleman.

474. *Chinese of moderate means.*

475. *Nobleman of southern Arabia.*

476. *Woman of southern Arabia.*

477. *Girl of the north Arabian desert.*

478. *Arab of the region bordering on the desert.*

480. *Man of the north Arabian desert.*

479. *"African girl in the Indies."*

AMERICA

481. *Peruvian.*

482. *Nobleman of Cuzco.*

483. *Peruvian soldier in battle.*

484. *Another Peruvian soldier in battle.*

485. Peruvian women.

486. Young men of Mexico (foreground)
and of the Yucatan.

487. Mexican nobleman.

488. Women of Mexico and Nicaragua.

489. *Indian idol discovered in 1587 in* "Virginia" (*east coast of North Carolina*).

490. A "*king*" *of Florida.*

491. A "*queen*" *of Florida.*

492. *Warrior of Florida.*

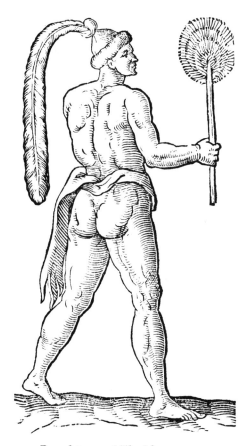

493. *Royal page of Florida.*

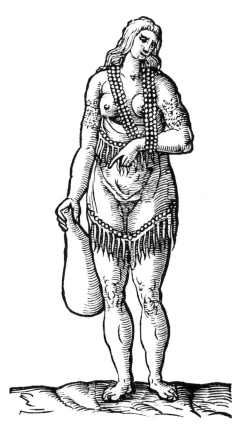

494. *Matrons and girls of Florida.*

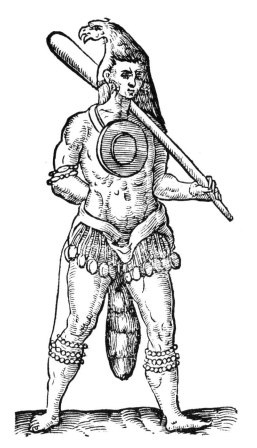

495. *Military officer of Florida.*

496. *Head of the camp, Florida.*

497. *Woman of "Virginia" (Roanoke colony).*

498. *Priest of the town of Secota, "Virginia."*

499. *One of the "chief lords" of Roanoke.*

500. *One of the "great lords of Virginia."*